ID0429469

Thoughts on
COURAGE

Thoughts on COURAGE

TRIUMPH BOOKS
CHICAGO

CONTENTS

INTRODUCTION

The moving motive in establishing FORBES Magazine, in 1917, was ardent desire to promulgate humaneness in business, then woefully lacking. . . .

Every issue of FORBES, since its inception, has appeared under the masthead: "With all thy getting, get understanding."

Not only so, but we have devoted, all through the years, a full page to "Thoughts on the Business of Life," reflections by ancient and modern sages calculated to inspire a philosophic mode of life, broad sympathies, charity towards all. . . .

I have faith that the time will eventually come when employees and employers, as well as all mankind, will realize that they serve themselves best when they serve others most.

B. C. Forbes

ACHIEVEMENT

Things done well
and with a care,
exempt themselves
from fear.

WILLIAM SHAKESPEARE

If you practice an art,
be proud of it
and make it proud of you . . .
It may break your heart,
but it will make you a person
in your own right.

MAXWELL ANDERSON

A determination to succeed
is the only way to succeed
that I know anything about.

WILLIAM FEATHER

Youth must be optimistic.
Optimism is essential
to achievement
and it is also the foundation
of courage
and of true progress.

NICHOLAS MURRAY BUTLER

A great part of courage
is having done the thing before.

RALPH WALDO EMERSON

Courage is virtue
only so far
as it is directed
to produce.

FRANÇOIS FÉNELON

A man is a lion
for his own cause.

SCOTTISH PROVERB

Man can have
but what he strives for.

ARABIAN PROVERB

Life is not easy for any of us.
But what of that?
We must have perseverance
and, above all,
confidence in ourselves.
We must believe
that we are gifted for something,
and that this thing,
at whatever cost,
must be attained.

MARIE CURIE

You can surmount the obstacles
in your path
if you are determined,
courageous and hard-working.
Never be fainthearted.
Be resolute,
but never bitter.
Permit no one to dissuade you
from pursuing the goals
you set for yourselves.
Do not fear to pioneer,
to venture down new paths of endeavor.

RALPH J. BUNCHE

Freedom dies
with every individual;
it is not reborn with his successors;
it must be achieved anew,
generation after generation.

HENRY M. WRISTON

Faith
that the thing can be done
is essential
to any great achievement.

THOMAS N. CARRUTHERS

It is the minority
that have stood in the van
of every moral conflict,
and achieved all that is noble
in the history of the world.

JOHN B. GOUGH

There are some things
one can only achieve
by a deliberate leap
in the opposite direction.
One has to go abroad
in order to find the home
one has lost.

FRANZ KAFKA

ADVERSITY

A pessimist is one
who makes difficulties
of his opportunities;
an optimist is one
who makes opportunities
of his difficulties.

REGINALD B. MANSELL

The block of granite
which was an obstacle
in the path of the weak,
becomes a stepping stone
in the path of the strong.

THOMAS CARLYLE

It is surmounting difficulties
that makes heroes.

LOUIS KOSSUTH

It is interesting to notice
how some minds
seem almost to create themselves,
springing up
under every disadvantage
and working their solitary
but irresistible way
through a thousand obstacles.

WASHINGTON IRVING

Difficulties are things
that show what men are.

EPICTETUS

Whatever you do,
you need courage.
Whatever course you decide upon,
there is always someone
to tell you you are wrong.
There are always difficulties arising
which tempt you to believe
that your critics are right.
To map out a course of action
and follow it to an end,
requires some of the same courage
which a soldier needs.
Peace has its victories,
but it takes brave men
to win them.

RALPH WALDO EMERSON

Courage,
it would seem,
is nothing less
than the power to overcome danger,
misfortune, fear, injustice,
while continuing to affirm inwardly
that life with all its sorrows
is good;
that everything is meaningful
even if in a sense
beyond our understanding;
and that there is always
tomorrow.

DOROTHY THOMPSON

Courage
conquers all things.

OVID

Adversity
has the effect
of eliciting talents
which in prosperous circumstances
would have lain dormant.

HORACE

He that can heroically
endure adversity
will bear prosperity
with equal greatness of soul;
for the mind that cannot be dejected
by the former
is not likely to be transported
with the latter.

HENRY FIELDING

The difficulties
and struggles
of today
are but the price
we must pay
for the accomplishments
and victories of tomorrow.

WILLIAM J. H. BOETCKER

Choose always the way
that seems the best,
however rough it may be;
custom will soon render it
easy and agreeable.

PYTHAGORAS

Accustom yourself
to master and overcome
things of difficulty;
for if you observe,
the left hand for want of practice
is insignificant,
and not adapted to general business,
yet it holds the bridle
better than the right,
from constant use.

PLINY

Undertake something
that is difficult;
it will do you good.
Unless you try to do something
beyond what you have already mastered,
you will never grow.

RONALD E. OSBORN

CHARACTER

A man must be strong enough
to mold the peculiarity
of his imperfections
into the perfection
of his peculiarities.

WALTER RATHENAU

⊷◆⊶

You cannot dream yourself
into a character;
you must hammer
and forge one
for yourself.

JAMES A. FROUDE

⊷◆⊶

Be kind;
every man you meet
is fighting a hard battle.

IAN MACLAREN

One man with courage
makes a majority.

ANDREW JACKSON

———◆———

Character
and personal force
are the only investments
that are worth anything.

WALT WHITMAN

———◆———

A decent boldness
ever meets with friends.

HOMER

There is nothing in the world
so much admired
as a man who knows
how to bear unhappiness
with courage.

SENECA

When a dog runs at you,
whistle for him.

HENRY DAVID THOREAU

The courage
of the tiger
is one,
and of the horse
another.

RALPH WALDO EMERSON

Anger is a prelude
to courage.

ERIC HOFFER

To be worth anything,
character must be capable
of standing firm upon its feet
in the world of daily work,
temptation, and trial.

SAMUEL SMILES

Great occasions
do not make heroes or cowards;
they simply unveil them
to the eyes of men.
Silently and imperceptibly,
as we wake or sleep,
we grow strong
or we grow weak,
and at last some crisis
shows us what we have become.

BISHOP WESCOTT

Good character
is that quality
which makes one dependable
whether being watched
or not,
which makes one truthful
when it is to one's advantage
to be a little less than truthful,
which makes one courageous
when faced with great obstacles,
which endows one
with the firmness
of wise self-discipline.

ARTHUR S. ADAMS

The brave man
carves out his fortune,
and every man
is the son of his own works.

MIGUEL DE CERVANTES

CONCERN

Do not accept trouble,
or worry about
what may never happen.
Keep in the sunlight.

BENJAMIN FRANKLIN

You'll break the worry habit
the day you decide
you can meet and master
the worst that can happen to you.

ARNOLD GLASOW

Worry,
whatever its source,
weakens,
takes away courage,
and shortens life.

JOHN LANCASTER SPALDING

To do anything in this world
worth doing,
we must not stand back shivering
and thinking of the cold and danger,
but jump in,
and scramble through
as well as we can.

SYDNEY SMITH

He that is overcautious
will accomplish little.

JOHANN SCHILLER

Too many people
are thinking of security
instead of opportunity.
They seem more afraid of life
than death.

JAMES F. BYRNES

Fear not
for the future,
weep not
for the past.

PERCY BYSSHE SHELLEY

It is a good rule
to face difficulties
at the time they arise
and not allow them to increase
unacknowledged.

EDWARD W. ZIEGLER

It is never safe
to look into the future
with eyes of fear.

E. H. HARRISON

A crowd of troubles passed him by
As he with courage waited;
He said, "Where do you troubles fly
When you are thus belated?"
"We go," they say, "to those who mope,
Who look on life dejected,
Who meekly say 'good-bye' to hope,
We go where we're expected."

FRANCIS J. ALLISON

To tremble
before anticipated evils,
is to bemoan
what thou hast never lost.

JOHANN WOLFGANG VON GOETHE

If you have a great ambition
take as big a step as possible
in the direction of fulfilling it,
but if the step is only a tiny one,
don't worry if it is the largest one
now possible.

MILDRED MCAFEE

Every tomorrow has two handles;
we can take hold
by the handle of anxiety
or by the handle of faith.

HENRY WARD BEECHER

The past cannot be changed,
the future is still in your power.

HUGH WHITE

CONFIDENCE

We make way
for the man
who boldly pushes past us.

CHRISTIAN BOVEE

The man who cannot
believe in himself
cannot believe
in anything else.
The basis of all integrity
and character
is whatever faith
we have in our own integrity.

ROY L. SMITH

"Know thyself"
means this,
that you get acquainted
with what you know,
and what you can do.

MENANDER

Do not attempt
to do a thing
unless you are sure of yourself;
but do not relinquish it
simply because someone else
is not sure of you.

STEWART E. WHITE

Confidence is a thing
not to be produced
by compulsion.
Men cannot be forced
into trust.

DANIEL WEBSTER

We are very much
what others think of us.
The reception our observations meet with
give us courage to proceed,
or dampen our efforts.

WILLIAM HAZLITT

The world has a habit
of giving what is demanded of it.
If you are frightened
and look for failure and poverty,
you will get them,
no matter how hard
you may try to succeed.
Lack of faith in yourself,
in what life will do for you,
cuts you off
from the good things
of the world.
Expect victory
and you make victory.
Nowhere is this truer
than in business life.

PRESTON BRADLEY

Be not afraid of life.
Believe that life is worth living,
and your belief
will help create the fact.

WILLIAM JONES

It isn't the size
of the dog in the fight,
but the size of the fight in the dog
that counts.

WOODY HAYES

The more people
who believe in something,
the more apt it is
to be wrong.
The person who's right
often has to stand alone.

SOREN KIERKEGAARD

Fight!
Be somebody!
If you have lost confidence
in yourself,
make believe
you are somebody else,
somebody that's got brains,
and act like him.

SOL HESS

Every man
who believes in himself,
no matter who he be,
stands on a higher level
than the wobbler.

HERMANN KEYSERLING

In the assurance of strength
there is strength;
and they are the weakest,
however strong,
who have no faith in themselves
or their powers.

CHRISTIAN BOVEE

To grow and know
what one is growing towards—
that is the source of all strength
and confidence in life.

JAMES BAILLIE

COWARDICE

Heaven never helps the man
who will not act.

SOPHOCLES

———

The people to fear
are not those
who disagree with you,
but those who disagree with you
and are too cowardly
to let you know.

NAPOLEON BONAPARTE

———

To live in the fear
of losing it
is to lose the point of life.

MALCOLM S. FORBES

If a man harbors
any sort of fear,
it percolates through
all his thinking,
damages his personality,
makes him landlord
to a ghost.

LLOYD C. DOUGLAS

———◆———

There is no advancement
to him who stands trembling
because he cannot see
the end from the beginning.

E. J. KLEMME

———◆———

The concessions of the weak
are the concessions of fear.

EDMUND BURKE

Because a fellow
has failed once or twice,
or a dozen times,
you don't want to set him down
as a failure
till he's dead
or loses his courage—
and that's the same thing.

GEORGE HORACE LORIMER

Only as a grand gesture of defeat
will men creep into the arms
of the state
and seek refuge
in its power
rather than their own courage.

HENRY M. WRISTON

True valor
lies in the middle,
between cowardice
and vulgar of the virtues.

MIGUEL DE CERVANTES

It is courage the world needs,
not infallibility . . .
courage is always
the surest wisdom.

WILFRED T. GRENFELL

Bravery escapes more dangers
than cowardice.

JOSEPH SEGUR

Some have been thought brave
because they were afraid
to run away.

THOMAS FULLER

———◆———

Except a person be part coward,
it is not a compliment
to say he is brave.

MARK TWAIN

———◆———

Many men spend their lives
in gazing at their own shadows,
and so dwindle away
into shadows thereof.

AUGUSTUS HARE

DANGER

Pugnacity is a form of courage,
but a very bad form.

SINCLAIR LEWIS

There is danger
in reckless change;
but greater danger
in blind conservatism.

HENRY GEORGE

The greatest asset
of any nation
is the spirit of its people,
and the greatest danger
that can menace any nation
is the breakdown of that spirit—
the will to win
and the courage to work.

GEORGE B. COURTELYOU

I would define true courage
to be a perfect sensibility
of the measure of danger,
and a mental willingness
to endure it.

WILLIAM TECUMSEH SHERMAN

Courage
is grace under pressure.

ERNEST HEMINGWAY

Courage in danger
is half the battle.

PLAUTUS

A ship in harbor is safe,
but that is not
what ships are built for.

JOHN SHEDD

The desire for safety
stands against every great
and noble enterprise.

TACITUS

This is the mark
of a really admirable man:
steadfastness
in the face of trouble.

LUDWIG VAN BEETHOVEN

Faced with crisis,
the man of character
falls back upon himself.

CHARLES DE GAULLE

If we survive danger
it steels our courage
more than anything else.

NIEBUHR

Men of courage,
they dared to go forward
despite all hazards.

THOMAS J. WATSON

Avoiding danger
is no safer in the long run
than outright exposure.
The fearful are caught
as often as the bold.
Faith alone defends.

HELEN KELLER

During the first period
of a man's life
the greatest danger is:
not to take the risk.
When once the risk
has really been taken,
then the greatest danger
is to risk too much.

SOREN KIERKEGAARD

DETERMINATION

So long as a man
still has inspiration
and the will to go on,
he still exemplifies youth.

MAURICE J. LEWI

—◆—

Never mind
what others do;
do better than yourself,
beat your own record
from day to day,
and you are a success.

WILLIAM J. H. BOETCKER

—◆—

It is a funny thing about life—
if you refuse to accept
anything but the best
you very often get it.

W. SOMERSET MAUGHAM

Determine to be
something in the world,
and you will be something.
"I cannot,"
never accomplished anything;
"I will try,"
has wrought wonders.

JOEL HAWES

A man can do his best
only by confidently seeking
(and perpetually missing)
an unattainable perfection.

RALPH BARTON PERRY

The man who ventures
to write contemporary history
must expect to be attacked
both for everything he has said
and everything he has not said.

FRANÇOIS-MARIE AROUET VOLTAIRE

I care not
what your education is,
elaborate or nothing,
what your mental caliber is,
great or small,
that man who concentrates
all his energies of body,
mind, and soul
in one direction
is a tremendous man.

T. DEWITT TALMAGE

Morale
is when your hands and feet
keep on working
when your head says
it can't be done.

BENJAMIN MORRELL

Failure
is only postponed success
as long as courage
"coaches" ambition.
The habit of persistence
is the habit of victory.

HERBERT KAUFMAN

To men
pressed by their wants
all change is ever welcome.

BEN JONSON

The greatest test of courage on earth
is to bear defeat
without losing heart.

ROBERT GREEN INGERSOLL

Rocks have been shaken
from their solid base,
but what shall move
a firm and dauntless mind?

JOANNA BAILLIE

When we see ourselves in a situation
which must be endured
and gone through,
it is best to make up our minds to it,
meet it with firmness,
and accommodate everything to it
in the best way practicable.

THOMAS JEFFERSON

FAITH

Faith
is not trying to believe something
regardless of the evidence,
faith
is daring to do something
regardless of the consequences.

SHERWOOD EDDY

———

Inflexible in faith,
invincible in arms.

JAMES BEATTIE

———

As the essence of courage
is to stake one's life
on a possibility,
so the essence of faith
is to believe
that the possibility exists.

WILLIAM SALTER

A man full of courage
is also full of faith.

CICERO

My message to you is:
Be courageous!
I have lived a long time.
I have seen history repeat itself
again and again.
I have seen many depressions
in business.
Always America has come out
stronger and more prosperous.
Be as brave
as your fathers before you.
Have faith!
Go forward.

THOMAS EDISON

If fear is cultivated
it will become stronger.
If faith is cultivated
it will achieve the mastery.
We have a right to believe
that faith is the stronger emotion
because it is positive
whereas fear is negative.

JOHN PAUL JONES

Courage
is worth nothing
if the gods withhold their aid.

EURIPIDES

In doubtful matters
courage may do much;
in desperate, patience.

THOMAS FULLER

Our doubts are traitors
and cause us to miss the good
we oft might win
by fearing to attempt.

WILLIAM SHAKESPEARE

Fate gave to man
the courage of endurance.

LUDWIG VAN BEETHOVEN

All the strength
and force of man
comes from his faith
in things unseen.
He who believes
is strong;
he who doubts
is weak.
Strong convictions
precede great actions.

JAMES FREEMAN CLARKE

———◆———

Faith gives the courage
to live and do.

ARTHUR H. COMPTON

No iron chain,
or outward force of any kind,
could ever compel
the soul of man
to believe or disbelieve.

THOMAS CARLYLE

I think we may safely trust
a good deal more
than we do.
We may waive
just so much care of ourselves
as we honestly bestow elsewhere.

HENRY DAVID THOREAU

In actual life
every great enterprise
begins with
and takes its first forward step
in faith.

FRIEDRICH VON SCHLEGEL

The only faith
that wears well
and holds its color
in all weathers
is that which is woven
of conviction.

JAMES RUSSELL LOWELL

FEAR

Valor grows by daring,
fear by holding back.

SYRUS

What the world has to eradicate
is fear and ignorance.

JAN MASARYK

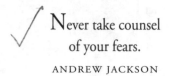

Never take counsel
of your fears.

ANDREW JACKSON

There is a courageous wisdom;
there is also a false reptile prudence,
the result, not of caution,
but of fear.

EDMUND BURKE

Fear is like fire:
If controlled
it will help you;
if uncontrolled,
it will rise up and destroy you.
Men's actions
depend to a great extent
upon fear.
We do things
either because we enjoy doing them
or because we are afraid
not to do them.

JOHN F. MILBURN

Half our fears
are baseless;
the other half
discreditable.

CHRISTIAN BOVEE

Courage
is a special kind of knowledge:
the knowledge of how to fear
what ought to be feared
and how not to fear
what ought not to be feared.

DAVID BEN-GURION

———⋗∘⋖———

The thing in the world
I am most afraid of
is fear.

RABINDRANATH TAGORE

———⋗∘⋖———

It is not death
that a man should fear,
but he should fear
never beginning to live.

MARCUS AURELIUS ANTONINUS

Nothing in life is to be feared.
It is only to be understood.

MARIE CURIE

Fear is an acid
which is pumped into one's atmosphere.
It causes mental, moral,
and spiritual asphyxiation,
and sometimes death;
death to energy and all growth.

HORACE FLETCHER

I thatched my roof
when the sun was shining,
and now I am not afraid of the storm.

GEORGE F. STIVENS

The worst sorrows in life
are not in its losses and misfortunes,
but its fears.

ARTHUR CHRISTOPHER BENSON

———

It is better to have a right destroyed
than to abandon it because of fear.

PHILLIP MANN

———

Fear never has led,
and never will lead,
a man victoriously
in any phase of life.

GEORGE MATTHEW ADAMS

———

Put fear out of your heart.

WILLIAM ALLEN WHITE

HONESTY

Unless the idealist
is brave
and has the courage
to face the truth,
his idealism creates nothing.

GRENVILLE KLEISER

The best kind of citizen
and the solidest kind of enterprise
is one that can look the whole world
in the face.

M. E. TRACY

We must dare to be happy,
and dare to confess it,
regarding ourselves always
as the depositories,
not as the authors
of our own joy.

HENRI FRÉDÉRIC AMIEL

Every man of courage
is a man of his word.

PIERRE CORNEILLE

Courage
is what it takes
to stand up and speak;
courage is also what it takes
to sit down and listen.

WINSTON S. CHURCHILL

The most sublime courage
I have ever witnessed
has been among that class
too poor to know
they possessed it,
and too humble for the world
to discover it.

GEORGE BERNARD SHAW

———◆———

Fear fades
when facts are faced.

FRANK TYGER

———◆———

The first step in handling anything
is gaining the ability to face it.

L. RON HUBBARD

Truth never hurts
the teller.

ROBERT BROWNING

He who knows no guilt
knows no fear.

PHILIP MASSINGER

Honest men fear
neither the light
nor the dark.

THOMAS FULLER

For truth and duty
it is ever the fitting time;
who waits until circumstances
completely favor his undertaking,
will never accomplish anything.

MARTIN LUTHER

All problems become smaller
if you don't dodge them,
but confront them.
Touch a thistle timidly,
and it pricks you;
grasp it boldly,
and its spine crumbles.

WILLIAM S. HALSEY

Hope knows not
if fear speaks truth,
nor fear
whether hope be blind as she.

ALGERNON CHARLES SWINBURNE

All truth is safe
and nothing else is safe;
and he who keeps back the truth,
or withholds it from men,
from motives of expediency,
is either a coward or a criminal
or both.

MAX MÜLLER

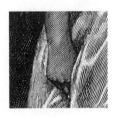

There are truths which are not
for all times
nor for all men.

FRANÇOIS-MARIE AROUET VOLTAIRE

Let us then be what we are,
and speak what we think,
and in all things
keep ourselves loyal
to truth.

HENRY WADSWORTH LONGFELLOW

HOPE

In the midst of winter,
I finally learned
that there was in me
an invincible summer.

ALBERT CAMUS

I steer my bark
with hope in the head,
leaving fear astern.

THOMAS JEFFERSON

If we would guide
by the light of reason
we must let our minds
be bold.

LOUIS D. BRANDEIS

Hope is the boy,
a blind, head-long
pleasant fellow,
good to chase swallows
with the salt;
Faith is the grave,
experienced,
yet smiling man.
Hope lives on ignorance;
open-eyed Faith
is built upon a knowledge
of our life,
of the tyranny
of circumstance
and the frailty
of human nature.

ROBERT LOUIS STEVENSON

Courage is the first
of human qualities
because it is the quality
which guarantees all the others.

WINSTON S. CHURCHILL

You cannot build
character and courage
by taking away a man's initiative
and independence.

WILLIAM J. H. BOETCKER

Whatever enlarges hope
will also exalt courage.

THOMAS FULLER

Nobody can really guarantee
the future.
The best we can do
is size up the chances,
calculate the risks involved,
estimate our ability
to deal with them
and then make our plans
with confidence.

HENRY FORD II

Courage is like love;
it must have hope
to nourish it.

NAPOLEON BONAPARTE

Hope
awakens courage.
He who can implant courage
in the human soul
is the best physician.

KARL LUDWIG VON KNEBEL

Whatever you can do,
or dream you can . . .
begin it;
boldness has genius,
power, and magic in it.

JOHANN WOLFGANG VON GOETHE

Not one of us
knows what effect
his life produces,
and what he gives to others;
that is hidden from us
and must remain so,
though we are often allowed
to see some little fraction of it,
so that we may not
lose courage.
The way in which power works
is a mystery.

ALBERT SCHWEITZER

There is no fear
without some hope,
and no hope
without some fear.

BARUCH SPINOZA

Hope is brightest
when it dawns from fears.

WALTER SCOTT

PERSEVERANCE

The strong man,
the positive, decisive man
who has a program
and is determined
to carry it out,
cuts his way to his goal
regardless of difficulties.
It is the discouraged man
who turns aside
and takes a crooked path.

ORISON SWETT MARDEN

I have lived long enough
to be battered
by the realities of life
and not too long
to be downed by them.

JOHN MASON BROWN

Courage and perseverance
have a magical talisman,
before which difficulties disappear
and obstacles vanish into air.

JOHN QUINCY ADAMS

I'm proof
against that word *failure*.
I've seen behind it.
The only failure
a man ought to fear
is failure in cleaving
to the purpose he sees to be
the best.

GEORGE ELIOT

Watch a man
with scrutiny
when his will is crossed,
and his desires disappointed.
The quality of spirit
he reveals at that time
will determine the character
of the man.

RICHARD T. WILLIAMS

It takes vision and courage
to create—
it takes faith and courage
to prove.

OWEN D. YOUNG

Courage to start
and willingness
to keep everlastingly at it
are the requisites for success.

ALONZO NEWTON BENN

Take heart again;
put your dismal fears away.
One day,
who knows?
Even these hardships
will be grand things
to look back on.

VIRGIL

A stout man's heart
breaks bad luck.

MIGUEL DE CERVANTES

And have you not
received faculties
which will enable you
to bear all
that happens to you?
Have you not received
greatness of spirit?
Have you not
received courage?
Have you not
received endurance?

EPICTETUS

⁘

We can do anything
we want to do
if we stick to it long enough.

HELEN KELLER

Have patience
with all things,
but chiefly have patience
with yourself.
Do not lose courage
in considering your own imperfections,
but instantly start remedying them—
every day begin the task anew.

ST. FRANCIS DE SALES

———

Braving obstacles and hardships
is nobler than retreat to tranquility.
The butterfly that hovers
around the lamp
until it dies
is more admirable
than the mole that lives
in the dark tunnel.

KAHLIL GIBRAN

The conditions of conquest
are always easy.
We have but to toil awhile,
endure awhile, believe always,
and never turn back.

SENECA

Perseverance
is more prevailing than violence;
and many things
which cannot be overcome
when they are together,
yield themselves up
when taken little by little.

PLUTARCH

PRINCIPLE

Men of principle
are always bold,
but those who are bold
are not always men
of principle.

CONFUCIUS

It is often easier
to fight for a principle
than to live up to it.

ADLAI STEVENSON

I count him braver
who overcomes his desires
than him who conquers his enemies;
for the hardest victory
is the victory over self.

ARISTOTLE

The test of tolerance
comes when we are in a majority;
the test of courage
comes when we are in a minority.

RALPH W. SOCKMAN

Too few
have the courage
of my convictions.

ROBERT M. HUTCHINS

Courage
is the most common and vulgar
of the virtues.

HERMAN MELVILLE

———

It is curious
that physical courage
should be so common
in the world,
and moral courage so rare.

MARK TWAIN

———

Courage
is the supreme virtue,
because it is the guarantor
of every other virtue.

BERGEN EVANS

Courage
is a quality so necessary
for maintaining virtue
that it is always respected,
even when it is associated
with vice.

SAMUEL JOHNSON

Physical courage,
which despises all danger,
will make a man brave
in one way;
and moral courage,
which despises all opinion,
will make a man brave
in another.

CHARLES CALEB COLTON

Physical bravery
is an animal instinct;
moral bravery
is a much higher
and truer courage.

WENDELL PHILLIPS

———

To see what is right,
and not do it,
is want of courage,
or of principle.

CONFUCIUS

———

When moral courage
feels that it is in the right,
there is no personal daring
of which it is incapable.

LEIGH HUNT

Aggressive fighting
for the right
is the greatest sport
in the world.

THEODORE ROOSEVELT

⁓⋅◆⋅⁓

Be unafraid
in all things
when you know
you are in the right.

CHARLES W. ELIOT

I do not regret
having braved public opinion,
when I knew it was wrong
and was sure
it would be merciless.

HORACE GREELEY

RESOLUTION

Courage
leads starward,
fear
toward death.

SENECA

⸺✦⸺

To have integrity
the individual cannot
merely be a weather vane
turning briskly
with every doctrinal wind
that blows.
He must possess key loyalties
and key convictions
which can serve
as a basis of judgment
and a standard of action.

JOHN STUDEBAKER

All brave men love;
for he only is brave
who has affections
to fight for,
whether in the daily battle of life,
or in physical contests.

NATHANIEL HAWTHORNE

Let us go forth
and resolutely dare
with sweat of brow
to toil our little day.

JOHN MILTON

Follow your own path,
no matter what people say.

KARL MARX

I neither complain of the past,
nor do I fear the future.

MICHEL DE MONTAIGNE

I love the man
who can smile in trouble,
that can gather strength
from distress,
and grow brave by reflection.
'Tis the business of little minds
to shrink,
but he whose heart is firm,
and whose conscience
approves his conduct,
will pursue his principles
unto death.

THOMAS PAINE

Necessity of action
takes away the fear of the act,
and makes bold resolution
the favorite of fortune.

FRANCIS QUARLES

You cannot run away
from a weakness.
You must sometimes
fight it out or perish;
and if that be so,
why not now,
and where you stand?

ROBERT LOUIS STEVENSON

There is nothing
more to be esteemed
than a manly firmness
and decision of character.
I like a person
who knows his own mind
and sticks to it;
who sees at once what,
in given circumstances,
is to be done,
and does it.

WILLIAM HAZLITT

The resolved mind
hath no cares.

GEORGE HERBERT

Be stirring as the time,
be fire with fire,
threaten the threatener,
and outface the brow
of bragging horror;
so shall inferior eyes,
that borrow their behaviors
from the great,
grow great by your example
and put on the dauntless spirit
of resolution.

WILLIAM SHAKESPEARE

You can't fly a kite
unless you go against the wind
and have a weight
to keep it from turning somersault.

WILLIAM J. H. BOETCKER

———◆———

There is no alleviation
for the sufferings of mankind
except veracity of thought and action,
and the resolute facing
of the world as it is.

THOMAS H. HUXLEY

RESPONSIBILITY

Where duty is plain,
delay is both foolish
and hazardous;
where it is not,
delay may be
both wisdom and safety.

TRYON EDWARDS

You can't escape
the responsibility of tomorrow
by evading it today.

ABRAHAM LINCOLN

No one can accept responsibility
in the world
unless he takes it first
on his own doorstep.

CLEO F. CRAIG

Every individual
has a place to fill in the world,
and is important
in some respect,
whether he chooses to be so
or not.

NATHANIEL HAWTHORNE

To save something
each month
develops self-control.
This power
frees one from fear
and gives abiding courage.

SAMUEL REYBURN

Moral courage
is a virtue of higher cast
and nobler origin
than physical.
It springs from
a consciousness of virtue
and renders a man,
in the pursuit or defense of right,
superior to the fear of reproach,
opposition in contempt.

SAMUEL GOODRICH

Courage
without conscience
is a wild beast.

RALPH INGERSOLL

Having the courage
to live within one's means
is respectability.

BENJAMIN DISRAELI

We should not forget
that our tradition
is one of protest and revolt,
and it is stultifying
to celebrate
the rebels of the past . . .
while we silence
the rebels of the present.

HENRY STEELE COMMAGER

Dishonesty, cowardice, and duplicity
are never impulsive.

GEORGE KNIGHT

There is nothing in the universe
that I fear,
but that I shall not know
all my duty,
or shall fail to do it.

MARY LYON

We are not altogether here
to tolerate.
We are here to resist,
to control
and vanquish withal.

THOMAS CARLYLE

This country
was not built by men
who relied on somebody else
to take care of them.
It was built by men
who relied on themselves,
who dared to shape
their own lives,
who had enough courage
to blaze new trails—
enough confidence in themselves
to take the necessary risks.

J. OLLIE EDMUND

It is not enough
to be ready to go
where duty calls.
A man should stand around
where he can hear the call!

ROBERT LOUIS STEVENSON

Take ground for truth,
and justice, and rectitude,
and piety, and fight well,
and there can be no question
as to the result.

HENRY WARD BEECHER

Do today's duty,
fight today's temptation;
do not weaken and distract yourself
by looking forward
to things you cannot see,
and could not understand
if you saw them.

CHARLES KINGSLEY

RISK

The bravest
are the tenderest.
The loving
are the daring.

HENRY WADSWORTH LONGFELLOW

———⊷⊶———

I would be brave,
For there is much to dare.

HOWARD A. WHEELER

———⊷⊶———

Dare
to go forward.

MAYER AMSCHEL ROTHSCHILD

Every noble acquisition
is attended with its risks;
he who fears
to encounter the one
must not expect
to obtain the other.

PIETRO METASTASIO

———

Any life truly lived
is a risky business,
and if one puts up
too many fences
against the risks
one ends up
shutting out life itself.

KENNETH S. DAVIS

Without risk,
faith is an impossibility.

SOREN KIERKEGAARD

To be alive at all
involves some risk.

HAROLD MACMILLAN

It is better
by a noble boldness
to run the risk of being subject
to half of the evils we anticipate,
than to remain
in cowardly listlessness
for fear of what may happen.

HERODOTUS

I find no foeman
in the road
but fear;
to doubt is failure
and to dare is success.

FREDERIC KNOWLES

Nothing
would be done at all
if a man waited
till he could do it so well
that no one could find fault with it.

CARDINAL JOHN HENRY NEWMAN

The will to do,
the soul to dare.

WALTER SCOTT

There is nothing more difficult
to take in hand,
more perilous to conduct,
or more uncertain in its success
than to take the lead
in the introduction
of a new order of things.

NICCOLÓ MACHIAVELLI

The men
who succeed best
in public life
are those who take the risk
of standing by
their own convictions.

JAMES A. GARFIELD

Nothing splendid
has ever been achieved
except by those
who dared believe
that something inside them
was superior to circumstance.

BRUCE BARTON

———

It is not enough
that you form,
and even follow
the most excellent rules
for conducting yourself
in the world;
you must, also,
know when to deviate
from them,
and where lies
the exception.

FULKE GREVILLE

The shell must break
before the bird can fly.

ALFRED TENNYSON

—◦◦◦—

No one knows
what it is that he can do
until he tries.

SYRUS

SACRIFICE

The mark
of the immature man
is that he wants to die nobly
for a cause,
while the mark
of the mature man
is that he wants to live humbly
for one.

WILLIAM STEKEL

Wherever humanity
has made that hardest
of all starts
and lifted itself out
of mere brutality
is a sacred spot.

WILLA CATHER

If appeasing our enemies
is not the answer,
neither is hating them . . .
Somewhere between the extremes
of appeasement and hate
there is a place
for courage and strength
to express themselves
in magnanimity
and charity,
and this is the place
we must find.

A. WHITNEY GRISWOLD

Courage consists
in equality to the problem
before us.

RALPH WALDO EMERSON

Happy is he
who dares courageously
to defend what he loves.

OVID

* * *

Often the test
of courage
is not to die
but to live.

VITTORIO ALFIERI

* * *

Why should we honor
those that die
upon the field of battle?
A man may show
as reckless a courage
in entering into the abyss
of himself.

WILLIAM BUTLER YEATS

It is an error
to suppose that courage
means courage in everything.
Most people are brave
only in the dangers
to which they accustom themselves,
either in imagination
or practice.

EDWARD GEORGE BULWER-LYTTON

Only those
are fit to live
who are not afraid
to die.

GENERAL DOUGLAS MACARTHUR

Set the allowance
against the loss
and thou shalt find
no loss great.

FRANCIS QUARLES

The wise man
does not expose himself needlessly
to danger,
since there are few things
for which he cares sufficiently;
but he is willing,
in great crises,
to give even his life—
knowing that under certain circumstances
it is not worthwhile to live.

ARISTOTLE

Fix your eyes
upon the greatness
of your country
as you have it before you
day by day . . .
and when you feel her great,
remember that her greatness
was won by men with courage,
with knowledge of their duty
and with a sense of honor in action,
who, even if they failed
in some venture,
would not think
of depriving their country
of their powers
but laid them at her feet
as their fairest offering.

PERICLES

I am the only one,
but still I am one;
I cannot do everything,
but still I can do something;
and because I cannot do everything
I will not refuse to do the something
that I can do.

EDWARD E. HALE

If you desire to be magnanimous,
undertake nothing rashly,
and fear nothing thou undertakest.
Fear nothing but infamy;
dare anything but injury;
the measure of magnanimity
is to be neither rash nor timorous.

FRANCIS QUARLES

STRENGTH

Live in terms
of your strong points.
Magnify them.
Let your weaknesses
shrivel up and die
from lack of nourishment.

WILLIAM YOUNG ELLIOTT

The strongest man in the world
is he who stands most alone.

HENRIK IBSEN

Oh! It is excellent
to have a giant's strength;
but it is tyrannous to use it
like a giant.

WILLIAM SHAKESPEARE

The individual activity
of one man with backbone
will do more than a thousand men
with a mere wishbone.

WILLIAM J. H. BOETCKER

Limit to courage?
There is no limit to courage.

GABRIELE D'ANNUNZIO

Don't foul,
don't flinch—
hit the line hard.

THEODORE ROOSEVELT

It takes courage to live—
courage and strength
and hope and humor.
And courage and strength
and hope and humor
have to be bought and paid for
with pain and work
and prayers and tears.

JEROME P. FLEISHMAN

There is no better sign
of a brave mind
than a hard hand.

WILLIAM SHAKESPEARE

He who is afraid of a thing
gives it power over him.

MOORISH PROVERB

That case is strong
which has, not a multitude,
but one strong man
behind it.

JAMES RUSSELL LOWELL

To be independent
is the business of a few only;
it is the privilege of the strong.

FRIEDRICH W. NIETZSCHE

The opinion of the strongest
is always the best.

JEAN DE LA FONTAINE

The human spirit
is stronger than anything
that can happen to it.

C. C. SCOTT

Don't hit at all
if it is honorably possible
to avoid hitting;
but never hit soft.

THEODORE ROOSEVELT

Because your own strength
is unequal to the task,
do not assume that it is beyond
the powers of man;
but if anything is within the powers
and province of man,
believe that it is within
your own compass also.

MARCUS AURELIUS ANTONINUS

Only a strong tree
can stand alone.

ARNOLD GLASOW

If thou wouldst conquer
thy weakness
thou must not gratify it.

WILLIAM PENN

He who reigns within himself,
and rules passions, desires, and fears,
is more than a king.

JOHN MILTON

Our country's honor calls upon us
for a vigorous and manly exertion;
and if we now shamefully fail,
we shall become infamous to the whole world.

GEORGE WASHINGTON

Although men are accused
of not knowing their own weakness,
yet perhaps few know their own strength.
It is in men as in soils,
where sometimes there is a vein of gold
which the owner knows not of.

JONATHAN SWIFT

Venture

After you've done a thing
the same way for two years,
look it over carefully.
After five years,
look at it with suspicion.
And after ten years,
throw it away and start all over.

ALFRED E. PERLMAN

⊸◆⊶

Without push,
pull's useless.

MALCOLM S. FORBES

⊸◆⊶

All men's gains
are the fruit
of venturing.

HERODOTUS

Why not go
out on a limb?
Isn't that where
the fruit is?

FRANK SCULLY

When you cannot
make up your mind
which of two evenly balanced
courses of action
you should take—
choose the bolder.

W. J. SLIM

Who bravely dares
must sometimes risk
a fall.

SMOLLETT

The difference between
getting somewhere
and nowhere
is the courage
to make an early start.
The fellow who sits still
and does just what he is told
will never be told
to do bigger things.

CHARLES M. SCHWAB

Put a grain of boldness
in everything you do.

BALTASAR GRACIÁN

He knew no fear
except the fear of doing wrong.

ROBERT GREEN INGERSOLL

———◆———

Who never climbs
rarely falls.

JOHN GREENLEAF WHITTIER

———◆———

Necessity
is the mother
of "taking chances."

MARK TWAIN

Look not sorrowfully
into the past;
it comes not back again.
Wisely improve
the present;
it is thine.
Go forth to meet
the shadowy future
without fear,
and with a manly heart.

HENRY WADSWORTH LONGFELLOW

Action
may not always bring
happiness,
but there is no happiness
without action.

BENJAMIN DISRAELI

Happiness comes only
when we push our brains
and hearts
to the farthest reaches
of which we are capable.

LEO ROSTEN

The most drastic
and usually the most effective
remedy for fear
is direct action.

WILLIAM BURNHAM

Either do not attempt at all,
or go through with it.

OVID

The fact is
to do anything in the world
worth doing,
we must not stand back shivering
and thinking of the cold and danger,
but jump in and scramble
through as well as we can.

RICHARD CUSHING

INDEX